KITE ISLAND

STORY AND ILLUSTRATIONS
BY ILONA HEMPERLY

Dedicated to my ohana *(family)*

© Ilona Hemperly 1992
Published by Aloha Island Art
Haleiwa Hawaii 96712

First Printing 1992
Second Printing 2015

Printed and bound in China

ISBN 978-0-9627294-3-0

On an island in Hawaii, stands the house where
Moki lives with his mother and father.

It is morning and Moki is working in the garden. He picks the seeds from the dried sunflowers. Some of the seeds he saves to grow more sunflowers and the rest he puts into his pockets to eat on today's adventure.

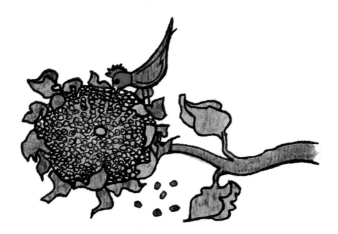

"I want to walk to Shell Bay to see Grandma and Grandpa," Moki tells his parents at breakfast. "I'm feeling lonely and you both are too busy to play with me."

"Shell Bay is over the Pali* on the other side of the island," protests Mother. "It is too far for you to walk alone."

"I'm alone now," sulks Moki. "I may as well be alone walking as sitting here."

"Now, Mama," says Moki's father. "Maybe a lonesome adventure is what the boy needs. I think he is ready to walk to Shell Bay and spend the night with Grandma and Grandpa. Come, Son, I'll walk with you as far as Swinging Bridge." "Mahalo*," says Moki.

*Pali – *mountain cliff*
*Mahalo – *thank you*

As they near the river gorge, Moki hears the hiss of the waterfall. He remembers that when he was little, the very thought of crossing Swinging Bridge made him feel dizzy. But now he is much older and braver. He says aloha* to his father and then runs heavily on his heels, rocking the bridge. His stomach starts to tingle.

"This is how it feels to climb a palm tree when I gather coconuts with father," gasps Moki in delight. In the center of the bridge, Moki looks back to see his smiling father still watching him. Moki grins and waves one last time, then turns and bounds away.

*aloha – *greeting of hello or goodbye*

Today Moki is boldhearted. He is going through the rainforest to the other side of the island, all by himself.

Trees and vines grow densely in the rainforest. Moki shields his eyes from low branches. Several times he trips on roots. He has been walking for hours. His skin and clothes are damp from the heat. Eventually he reaches the spring where he stops to rest and nibble sunflower seeds. He offers some seeds to a red bird, but it is frightened and flies away. Moki shudders, suddenly sensing his isolation. Then he laughs. "I'm more lonely now than I was this morning. I'm glad I will be seeing Grandma and Grandpa soon."

When Moki starts off again, he sees that there are several paths. "Which is the one that leads to Grandfather's house?" he wonders. He chooses the way that seems to head toward Shell Bay. Everything looks familiar and yet nothing looks exactly as he remembers it. Moki walks faster. The birds have stopped their chatter. It is getting dark.

"I'm lost," moans Moki. He remembers a lesson his father taught him and decides to make a shelter and gather some food while there is still a bit of light.

He cuts two elephant ear leaves for blankets and constructs a soft, dry bed of ferns. He collects bananas and lilikoi* for supper. The forest is very still. Moki snuggles into his leafy bed. Soon he is fast asleep.

*lilikoi – *passion fruit*

It is not until the morning sun coaxes his eyelids apart that he realizes how close to the beach he is. Moki bolts makai* down the trail and bursts into a clearing. There before him is Shell Bay. A solitary surfer is riding a wave. Beyond, on the arm of land that hugs Shell Bay, is his grandparent's cottage. Calling and waving, Moki runs into the garden where he sees Grandmother bending over her cabbages.

*makai – *direction toward the sea*

"Moki! Moki! What a surprise!" exclaims Grandmother, standing and wiping her hands on her skirt. "Where is your father? What! You walked here all by yourself? How wonderful that you came to spend the day with us. Go and find Grandpa. He is chopping wood for a new carving. I know he will be glad to see you, too."

Grandfather claps his hands and laughs. "Moki! I was sitting here wishing I had some help and surprise! Here you are! What shall we make today!"

Moki thinks carefully. "Could we build a kite, Grandpa?"

"Oh, so it's a kite you want. We can make a kite that will fly to the sun," chuckles Grandfather, reaching for some thick, bamboo sticks.

While they are working on the kite, Moki chews on dried Ahi* and coconut and tells Grandfather about his adventure. "I started out feeling lonely. But by the time night came and the birds stopped singing, it seemed as if there was no one in the world but me."

*Ahi – *yellow fin tuna fish*

Grandfather grins and hugs Moki with one hand, holding the finished kite with the other. "Even when you are alone, you are never really alone, little island boy. You always have your best friend with you."

Kneeling down, Grandfather whispers softly in Moki's ear. "You know who your best friend is, don't you?"

Moki's eyes grew large and questioning. "You, Grandpa...?" "No!" laughs Grandfather jumping up and pulling Moki's ear. "He's you!" They both laugh. "Where can we try out this new kite?" asks Grandfather. Moki answers, "I'd like to take it to the little island in Shell Bay where there are not so many trees to get in the way."

Grandfather must tend to his nets, but he agrees to let Moki use the boat. "Look!" says Grandfather handing Moki the oars. "There is a rainbow over Shell Bay. Something special will happen today."

When a giant sea turtle and beautiful kihikihi* swim right up to his boat, Moki decides this day will be very special indeed.

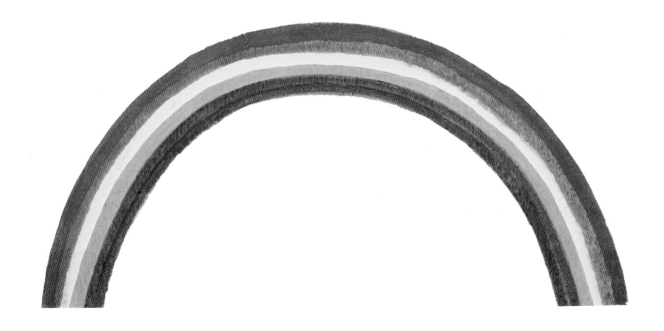

*kihikihi – *moorish idol fish*

The trade winds are strong today. Moki no sooner launches his new kite than a sudden gust pulls the string from his grasp, sending the kite to the top of the island's only coconut tree.

"Oh, no! What luck! I'll never get it down," wails Moki. "I wish Grandpa were here. He'd know what to do."

Then Moki remembers what Grandfather said about being his own best friend. "I know what to do and I can do it myself," declares Moki, not quite feeling the confidence of his words.

Slowly, Moki inches up the tree. "If I can climb a tree to pick coconuts, I should be able to climb a tree to get my kite," he is saying to himself. But the kite is not behaving like a coconut. It careens and taunts him, just out of reach. The tree sways, Moki sees the ground spin below. He closes his eyes and takes a deep breath. Time after time he stretches his arm toward the kite.
Now his fingers are crawling closer to its tail. Ah ha! He has it!

As soon as he's safely back on the ground, Moki clutches the string tightly and releases the kite to the wind. Flushed from the exhilaration of what he has done, Moki makes excited plans.

"I can't wait to show Mother and Father my new kite, although this island is the best place to fly it. There is so much open space here. It is a perfect kite island. That's what I'll call it! Kite Island!"

Relaxing, Moki lies back to look at his kite soaring alone, tugging gaily on its string.

Then Moki sees Grandfather standing alone with his net at the water's edge and feels another kind of tug.

"We are each alone," muses Moki. But there are also strings that tie us together. Right now I'm by myself on Kite Island. But soon I will be going back across the water through the rainforest, over Swinging Bridge, to a beach where my parents are alone, waiting for me.